They Call Me
Sacagawea

Joyce Badgley Hunsaker

TWODOT®

GUILFORD, CONNECTICUT
HELENA, MONTANA
AN IMPRINT OF THE GLOBE PEQUOT PRESS

Introduction

Two hundred years ago, President Thomas Jefferson sent Meriwether Lewis, William Clark, and their U.S. Army "Corps of Discovery" in search of the most direct and practical river route from the "U.States" to the Pacific Ocean. He charged them with finding reliable and economic routes for commerce. He also wanted information: scientific, cultural, and cartographic. Jefferson was sending the Corps where, truly, no white man had gone before.

It was during the winter of 1804–1805 that Lewis and Clark's paths crossed that of the teenaged Sacagawea. It was at Fort Mandan that Sacagawea stepped from her ordinary tribal life among her adopted Hidatsa people and into our history books. She did not seek out a special place in history. Instead, it seems that history sought her.

Many people have heard of Sacagawea, the young Shoshone mother who carried her baby across two thousand miles of wilderness—and back—on the Lewis and Clark Expedition. Yet few know who she was, as a person. Scholars cannot even agree on how to spell her name.

Sacagawea was an ordinary tribal woman who led an extraordinary life, not only during her trek with the Corps of Discovery, but from the time when, as a young girl, she was taken from the Shoshone by those Lewis and Clark called "Minnetaree." Tribal accounts of the Bird Woman give us insight into her resourcefulness, her inner strength, how she related to others, and what she thought during her life. Written accounts from the Expedition journals view her through her actions—impressions recorded

Tribal accounts of the Bird Woman give us insight into her resourcefulness.

by men outside her culture who could not even speak the same languages Sacagawea spoke.

To clearly understand what really happened in her life and why, we must listen to the stories of the Elders. We must search the written records of that long-ago time. We must learn the lessons of the land she lived upon and later crossed.

Sacagawea had strengths and weaknesses, just as we do. She sometimes made mistakes and had regrets. She endured the unimaginable and surmounted the impossible. Her life left its imprint on history. Her life leaves its imprint on us today.

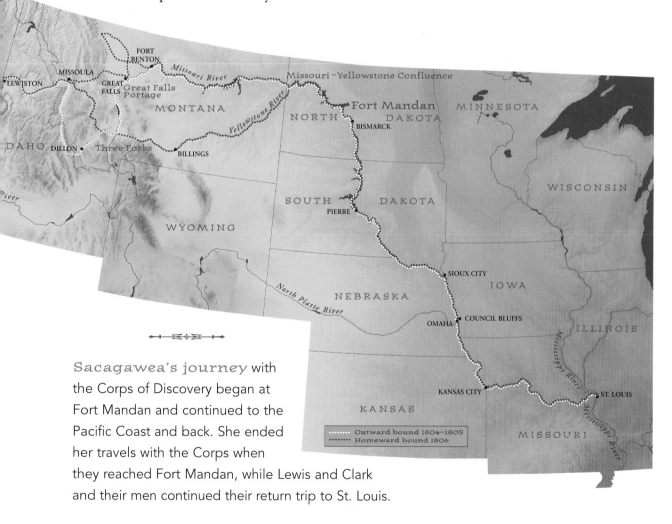

Sacagawea's journey with the Corps of Discovery began at Fort Mandan and continued to the Pacific Coast and back. She ended her travels with the Corps when they reached Fort Mandan, while Lewis and Clark and their men continued their return trip to St. Louis.

Some say my name is Sah-KAH-gah-WEE-ah. Some say SACK-ah-ja-WEE-ah. Still others, Tsa-KAH-kah-WEE-ah, or Sah-KAH-joo-ah. My own husband rarely called me the same name twice, usually settling for "Squaw," "Woman," or just "You." Chiefs Lewis and Clark did the same, but they added "Janey" because it was easy for their tongues to say. And when they named a river for me, they called it Bird Woman's River.

When my son was born, though, among my birth clan I became a new name: "Mother of Pomp." That is how I have thought of myself ever since.

I was born among the Numa Agui Dika, the "Salmon Eaters," sometimes called the "Snakes" from the Shoshoni hand sign that was misunderstood by the white men. To us, the sign looked like the tail of the salmon as it swam upstream. To the whites, the sign looked like the motion of a snake. So they called us Snake, or Shoshone.

There were many small bands of us in those days—each having clans—scattered across the land. I learned the ways of my people as all young girls do, under the watchful eyes of the Elders. All the women of my clan I called "mother," "sister," "grandmother." All the men, I called "father," "brother," "grandfather." This is how we were known to each other in the old days.

Sacagawea makes the hand sign for her people. The hand sign mistaken for "snake" has also been described as the motion involved in basket weaving, at which the Shoshones excelled. As in so many other things, the name sign used by this tribe was misunderstood by people outside the tribe. [LIZ HAHN PHOTO.]

Every year we traveled beyond the Beaverhead, following the buffalo, elk, and deer. I was old enough to have my own root-digging stick, old enough to scrape hides, old enough to be promised in marriage (about eleven snows) when those Lewis and Clark called "Minnetarees" raided our buffalo camp at the Three Forks, and I was taken.

I saw many of my people killed that day: four men, four women, most all of the boys. Some were able to escape into the trees. But me, they took, as they took most all the young girls. So it was that I came to live as a slave among the Minnetarees at the village of Awatixa on the Big River Missouri.

To the whites, the sign looked like the motion of a snake. So they called us Snake, or Shoshone.

Sacagawea makes the sign of the buffalo and the elk—two of the animals her people followed across the prairies and hunted for food and other necessities. [LIZ HAHN PHOTOS.]

5

One day I discovered that my friend, Naya Nuki, had escaped. I knew she would try to find our people. But the way was too long. The dangers were too many. I thought she would be recaptured and punished, or she would never find our people, and she would die alone in the mountains, with no one to grieve for her. No one to do ceremony. So I stayed.

I was made to work very hard. I learned to plant corn, beans, and squash. I learned to tend the growing things and to harvest. I learned to mound up earth and trees in a big circle to make a lodge different from the lodges of my people. And I learned the language.

When a girl child was born, it was common for an elder woman in her clan to give her a symbol of the valuable work the child would contribute to her family and tribe throughout her life—a child-sized root-digging stick. As a little girl, she would use this smaller version to imitate the work she saw the elder women perform. When she attained full adulthood, the young woman would receive another digging stick; this digging stick and subsequent others were used throughout her married life and sometimes passed down to others in her family.

[COURTESY USDA FOREST SERVICE, LEWIS AND CLARK NATIONAL HISTORIC TRAIL INTERPRETIVE CENTER, GREAT FALLS, MONTANA.]

It was not an unbearable life. In many ways, it was better than the life I had known with my people. Here, there was always more food, less hunger. Here, strange-looking and strange-sounding men from the trading companies traveled up and down the Big River, bringing skins, iron cooking pots, corn grinders, ribbons and beads, axes, traps, and guns. Best of all, they brought stories of what they had seen and who they had traded with. Here, there were Mandan, Minnetaree (also called "Big Bellies"), Arikara, Assiniboine, Cree, and more.

It was a life of interest. A life of plenty. I became content.

Bird's Eye View of the Mandan Village 1800 Miles above St. Louis. Oil painting by George Catlin, circa 1827–1839. One of several along the Knife River at its juncture with the Missouri, this Mandan village would have felt familiar to Sacagawea. The related Minnetaree villages were close neighbors. The rounded, earth-mound lodges served not only to keep the weather out but also as vantage points from which to view the village. On the roofs were stored "bull boats," so named for the bull buffalo hides stretched over willow frames to form the characteristic cuplike shape.

[COURTESY NATIONAL MUSEUM OF AMERICAN ART, SMITHSONIAN INSTITUTION. GIFT OF MRS. JOSEPH HARRISON, JR.]

The years came. The years went.

After a time, I was adopted into a Minnetaree clan and given the name by which you know me: Sacagawea. On that day, I was given a "woman's belt" made by the other women. Mine had blue beads on it, the sign of an industrious worker. It was hoped I would marry into the tribe, for then my husband would be honor-bound to provide meat not only for me, but for the rest of my new clan. Such was the custom in those days.

So how it was that I became the wife of a mixed-blood Frenchman, I cannot say. Some say it was a game of chance. Some say a bet or a trade. Some say he just took me. In the end, it did not matter how it happened. It all turned out the same. Toussaint Charbonneau became my husband. (It was said of him that he was always marrying someone!) I was barely fourteen snows.

The **blue beads** given to Sacagawea in her woman's belt were highly prized. The belt itself was a gift of honor. A woman could neither trade for nor make one for herself; no direct blood relative could give her one. The belt had to come from the other women of the clan. That an adoptive member would be given this honor speaks highly of Sacagawea's early training and her personal character. [LIZ HAHN PHOTO.]

I moved into his lodge at the Second Village, where I joined another of his wives and their son, also named Toussaint. Like me, Otter Woman was of the Snake tribe, but she was older than I. She had been with Charbonneau for many years. I was glad there would be two of us in the lodge to share the work.

I wondered if Otter Woman still remembered the words of Numa, our birth people. But Charbonneau did not like to hear Shoshoni spoken. He could not understand the words. No! In his lodge, he told us, we would speak only the Minnetaree, or Hidatsa, such as he spoke, and the few words of French that he would teach us. That was all we needed to know.

Mandan Earth Lodge (Interior), an engraving with aquatint by Karl Bodmer (circa 1839). Often measuring up to forty feet across, Mandan lodges provided ample space to stable horses and kennel dogs without encroaching upon human living space. The lodge also functioned as an informal meeting place, a workshop, nursery, kitchen, hotel, and storage facility. A central fire—ventilated through a smoke hole in the lodge roof—was screened from the entrance by upright logs, or puncheons, set in a trench for stability. The floor was tamped earth. Beds of buffalo robes were constructed to sit up off the floor, much like today's bed frames; many were enclosed by hides that hung from poles. The Mandan considered their lodges to belong to the women of the household. [Courtesy State Historical Society of North Dakota.]

When Lewis and Clark brought their men to our villages on the Big River, it was The Time of the Fallen Leaves. Geese were already flying south. The smells of snow and warming fires were on the wind.

They smoked the pipe with the head men of all the tribes. They made many speeches and gave many gifts. Lights danced in the northern skies, which they took for a good sign, so they decided to stay through the winter.

The first thing they did was to cut down the trees. They built rows of "houses," as they called them, made from "logs." But these houses sat flat against one another in straight lines, not rounded as a lodge should be—not round, as a village should be. Then they put up a high wall around their houses, closed the gate, and called it Fort Mandan.

The Palisade at Fort Mandan (reconstruction pictured) was laid out on a triangular pattern, the base of which formed the entrance wall. Living quarters adjoined one another on both sides of the triangle, meeting in back at the point where a guard tower was constructed. Each room likely contained a crude fireplace, a necessity in winter temperatures that commonly dipped below zero degrees Fahrenheit.
[COURTESY OF THE NORTH DAKOTA LEWIS AND CLARK BICENTENNIAL FOUNDATION.]

10

We were all curious about the white men. We wondered what was so important they had to keep it locked up inside the wall. It was said they had a big black dog, almost as big as a bear! And a big black man, almost as big as a tree! Charbonneau said his name was York. He was the slave of the red-haired chief, Clark. I thought this very strange, for no tribe I knew took men as slaves, only young women and girl children. The men, they killed, as befitted warriors. But Charbonneau said it was not the same among the whites. Some men owned other men.

The black man, York, was Big Medicine. The chiefs of all the villages tried to rub his blackness off, like dirt. But it would not come off. Then they felt of his hair, which was rough like the hair of the buffalo.

"He is a different animal than the whites," they said. Then all the People wanted to touch York, to become part of him and his Medicine.

Smoking of the pipe:

This was a ceremonial event. Tribes had distinctive ceremonies and formalities associated with presentation of the pipe. Men treasured their individual pipes, often decorating them with elaborate, sometimes symbolic ornamentation. Some pipes might be used for only the most sacred or serious circumstances; others might be smoked every day.

Sacagawea makes the sign of the dog. Before horses came to the People, dogs were used to pull loads and carry burdens. The sign for dog shows the two poles of the travois. The fingers are pulled toward the signer, just as the poles would have been pulled by the dogs. [LIZ HAHN PHOTO.]

Charbonneau said the white chiefs wanted to find a river way to the Big Water Where the Sun Goes Down. They needed guides and interpreters to speak for them with those whose homelands they would cross. They would pay well. So Charbonneau began going to the fort every day to talk with one of their interpreters who spoke French, as he did.

Then one day Charbonneau told Otter Woman and me that he would be going with Lewis and Clark and their men when they left in the spring. "Begin making moccasins and clothing for me!" he ordered. "I will be gone a very long time—longer than I have ever been gone before."

This elkskin shirt with quillwork (reproduction pictured) is of a style adopted by the Corps of Discovery for its comfort and durability. The style and ornamentation are typical of the Lewis-and-Clark-contact era. Porcupine quills have been dyed, flattened, and sewn onto the shirt, and additional designs painted over the chest and arm sections. The long fringe was mostly ornamental but could be used as tying material if the necessity arose. A shirt like this would probably have taken two medium-sized deer hides to create. The leather was wood-smoked, which served two purposes: It overrode all scent of man, and it added oils and resins that served to waterproof the leather.

[Courtesy USDA Forest Service, Lewis and Clark National Historic Trail Interpretive Center, Great Falls, Montana.]

He questioned us about our birth people, the Snakes. Where was their homeland? Would they be friendly to the whites? Did they have horses as he had heard? And could the whites trade with them for those horses so they could cross the Shining Mountains?

Otter Woman came from a different band than mine. It had been many snows since she had seen them or even thought about them. But my people, the Agui Dika, lived where Lewis and Clark wanted to go. Yes, I knew they had horses. Would they trade? This I did not know, for trading horses was something the men did, not the women.

And I could not say if they would be friendly to the whites. They had never seen one before, as far as I knew. I had not . . . not until I came here, to the Big River.

Then Charbonneau asked if I remembered the words, the words of Agui Dika—Shoshoni. Could I speak the words again? It had been so long since I had been allowed to speak them! But, oh yes, I remembered.

"Then you will come with me!" Charbonneau ordered. "Your people will speak to you in Shoshoni. You will say the words to me in Hidatsa, and I will say the words to someone else in French. Then that man will say the words in English for Lewis and Clark to understand."

I did not want to go. I was big and slow and awkward—with child. I did not know when the baby would come. I wanted to stay here, with Otter Woman.

Charbonneau said it did not matter. A woman with a baby would be a good sign. It would show, at a glance, that the Corps of Discovery was not a war party. Then he told me to gather our belongings. We were moving inside the fort.

He said nothing about Otter Woman and their son, Toussaint, coming with us. We knew, by his silence, they would be left behind for our Minnetaree relatives to look after.

When my time for birthing came, the pains started in the night. Lewis and Clark had ordered the gates of Fort Mandan closed every night at sundown and kept barred until morning. So Otter Woman was not with me to help bring the baby. The labor was long and hard. I was exhausted by the pain. I thought I might not live to see morning if the baby did not come soon.

A woman with a baby would be a good sign. It would show, at a glance, that the Corps of Discovery was not a war party.

Native "medicine pouches" carried items of powerful personal significance, not drugs.
[TERRY MCGREW PHOTO. MCGREW PHOTOGRAPHY.
© JOYCE BADGLEY HUNSAKER AND TOWANDA, INC.]

Finally, someone sent for Lewis. He and Clark had been making medicine on many in the villages throughout the winter. Maybe there was something in his pills and powders for me? But no, not for childbirth.

Then the interpreter Jussome, whose family lived in the Mandan village, said the rattle of snake would make the baby come. I could see by the face of Lewis, he did not think so. But he had such a rattle.

"Break it between your fingers," Jussome told Lewis. "Mix it with water, then make her drink."

I drank. Within minutes, my son was born!

"His name will be Jean Baptiste," shouted Charbonneau. "Named after my father!"

But to me, my son would always be Pomp, meaning "first-born" in the language of the Agui Dika.

The medicine chest Lewis brought on the expedition was probably very much like this one belonging to President Thomas Jefferson. Though Jefferson's kit shows a good number of glass bottles with stoppers, Lewis's Expedition inventory lists only three small bottles. Lewis tried to anticipate quantities and kinds of medicines the Corps of Discovery would need during their journey. He brought teas, powdered barks, heavy oils, exotic spices, and other remedies of the day. He also included several small medical instruments.

[COURTESY MONTICELLO AND THOMAS JEFFERSON MEMORIAL FOUNDATION. BY KIND PERMISSION OF MRS. PRENTICE COOPER.]

The next moon, ice began to snap and crack on the river. It was no longer safe to walk across the ice between the villages. I finished the cradleboard of willows I was making for Pomp. By then, boys could no longer make a game of jumping between floating pieces of ice from bank to bank. A few weeks more, and the river was flowing free. It was time to leave.

The long, flat canoes—called pirogues—were loaded with as many goods as they could carry: boxes, bundles of papers, instruments, books. There was barely enough room to sit. Sometimes Lewis's dog would run along the riverbank. Sometimes he would swim. Sometimes he would try to climb inside the boats! I carried Pomp in the cradleboard or in a sling made of skins on my back.

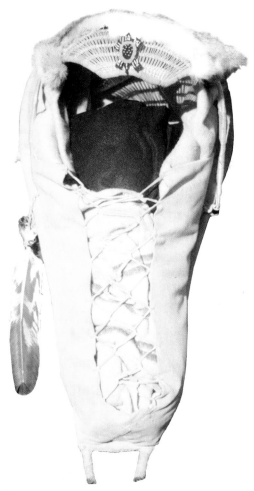

The frame of this traditional Shoshoni cradleboard is made from willows and covered with hide. The distinctive willow visor could be covered with rabbit fur in winter (as shown), or kept open in summer to shade the infant's face. Cradleboards were typically carried on the mother's back, either with a chest band or a band across her forehead, but they could also be leaned up against a tree or rock by means of the rest, or "foot" section. The style of cradleboard that Sacagawea would have made for Pomp is unknown. [Joyce Badgley Hunsaker photo.]

All the men took turns with the boats, even Charbonneau, who could not swim. He was steering our boat when the wind gusted against us so hard it almost tipped us over. If the sail had not caught on the water, we all would have been thrown into the river. Waves spilled over the side, into the boat. My brave husband panicked until the fiddleman, Cruzatte, pointed a pistol at him and told him to regain his senses or be shot.

Two of the men started scooping water out of the boat with kettles. Three others tried to row us to the bank. Pomp was safe on my back. Then I saw things start to float away, down the river. I did what anyone would do; I grabbed them as they passed me and pulled them back into the boat. A few things of great weight sank, but in the end, very little was lost.

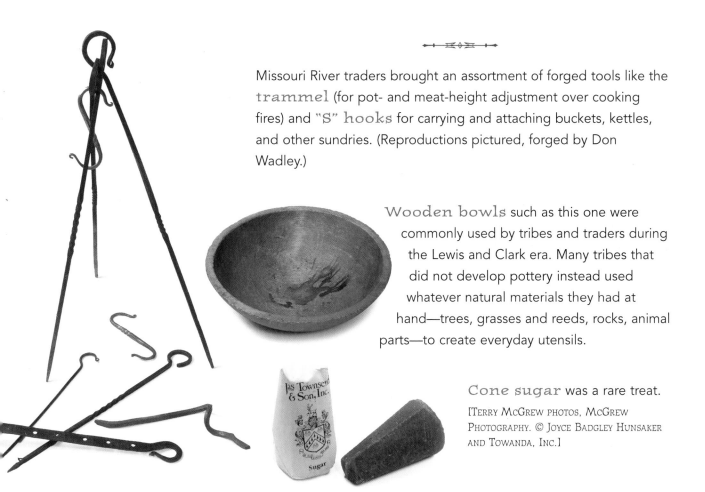

Missouri River traders brought an assortment of forged tools like the trammel (for pot- and meat-height adjustment over cooking fires) and "S" hooks for carrying and attaching buckets, kettles, and other sundries. (Reproductions pictured, forged by Don Wadley.)

Wooden bowls such as this one were commonly used by tribes and traders during the Lewis and Clark era. Many tribes that did not develop pottery instead used whatever natural materials they had at hand—trees, grasses and reeds, rocks, animal parts—to create everyday utensils.

Cone sugar was a rare treat.
[Terry McGrew photos, McGrew Photography. © Joyce Badgley Hunsaker and Towanda, Inc.]

One day went into the next . . . and the next . . . and the next. The men killed buffalo, antelope, and bear. The dog was bitten on the leg by a beaver and almost died, but Lewis worked his medicine on the wound and the dog lived.

We stopped with many tribes, where the men would smoke their pipes and say their speeches. They talked about the Great Father Jefferson and the need for peace among his "yellow Indian children." They gave medals to the head men with the face of the Great Father on one side and two hands clasping on the other. It was said that hands clasped in friendship could not be raised against one another in war.

They traded for buckskins, parfleches, quillwork, and shields to take back to the Great Father. They pulled out their writing desks and made marks in their journals. Each day brought us closer to the Shining Mountains and the need for horses. More and more often, the canoes could no longer travel the shrinking rivers. They had to be carried, or "portaged."

The tradition of giving peace medallions to important tribal chiefs was established in this country by the Spanish, French, and British, who made the first contacts with native peoples. It was common for medallions or medals to bear the likeness of the visitors' head of state. The Corps of Discovery's inventory rosters show medals of five sizes. Some displayed Jefferson's profile, others, figures of George Washington's administration. Some were silver, some bronze, and some medals were simply U.S. coins with a ring attached or a hole bored into them to accommodate a neck ribbon.

This particular piece (reproduction pictured) shows the profile of President Thomas Jefferson on the face, with the inscription, "TM. JEFFERSON PRESIDENT OF THE U.S. A.D.1801." The back of the medal shows a tomahawk and (peace) pipe above two clasped hands. The inscription reads, "PEACE AND FRIENDSHIP."

[TERRY MCGREW PHOTO, MCGREW PHOTOGRAPHY. © JOYCE BADGLEY HUNSAKER AND TOWANDA, INC.]

Soon, the captains grew anxious. Each time we would find the remains of a camp or the sign of a party that had passed, they would ask Charbonneau, "Are these her people?" Are these the Snakes? We need those horses!"

Near the place of the Buffalo Jump they found worn-out moccasins in a deserted camp site and had me "read" them. No, these were not the shape or decoration of the Agui Dika.

In order to keep a journal while on the expedition, ink powder first had to be mixed with water. The entries were written with quill pens. Only certain quills maintained their shape when cut to a pen "nib"; goose quills were considered the best. Lap desks of this period were hinged between lid and base so they could lie flat to provide an adequate writing surface. A storage compartment in the base held writing supplies and a small knife to sharpen quill nibs.

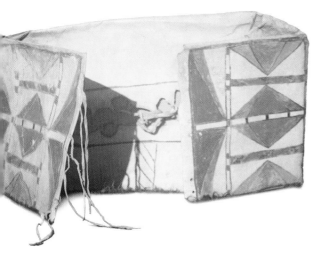

The parfleche—or animal hide suitcase—was in use by native peoples long before the advent of the Corps of Discovery. The hide's hair was singed off with fire and the hide scraped with hand tools until smooth. After proper curing, the resulting leather was shaped and decorated with mineral paints. Spread flat and open, the parfleche (a French word meaning "of skin") could accommodate a number of items. The sides were then folded in and tied. Finally, the ends were folded over and those, too, were tied.

[Joyce Badgley Hunsaker photos.]

The way grew harder. Holes, called caches, were dug in the ground. Here, the white men buried supplies so their loads would be lighter. They pulled the canoes over the ground with ropes wrapped over their shoulders. Sometimes we carried the burdens on our backs—even the captains.

I thought the great black dog would be made to pack supplies, too, but this did not happen. He helped bring down game for us to eat and barked at strange noises in the night, which woke us to danger, but I never saw him work in the way dogs were expected to work at the Mandan villages. Lewis, especially, treated him with much affection.

The way grew harder still. Our feet were cut and bruised by stones. Sharp spines pierced our skin, even through our moccasins. Then, at the Time of the Long Grass, I began to feel sick. At first I felt heavy and dull. Then came the fever. Lewis cut me, trying to bleed the sickness from me. But it did no good. Then he wrapped me in poultices of tree bark and made me drink opium tea.

Statue of Seaman (in Seaside, Oregon): Lewis's faithful Newfoundland dog was equally at home in water or on land. The breed is well known for its strength, endurance, intelligence, and sweet disposition. Seaman stood guard in camp at night, brought down wild game, and became a much-loved member of the Expedition. [DAVID B. HUNSAKER PHOTO.]

For days I was out of my head, walking among the spirits. My heart would race, then slow to nothing, then race again. My hands and arms trembled like leaves in a storm.

Finally, Lewis made me drink water from a stinking spring.

"Sulphur," he said. Again and again, he made me drink until I slept. The next morning, I woke. I knew who I was. And I was hungry!

But they fed me only buffalo broth, saying I had almost died. They said I was too weak for food. One day passed, then two days. Still, only buffalo broth with a few tiny pieces of meat to eat. I asked again and again for more.

On the third day, I was still hungry. So I waited until no one was looking, and I slipped away from camp. I found some breadroot to dig. "Prairie apples," they are called. Even though I knew they were not ready for digging, I ate them anyway. I ate and ate and ate and ate, until I was no longer hungry.

That night my stomach thundered and I was in terrible pain. My fever returned. Lewis was very angry.

"Too many raw 'apples,' Janey! And too little sense!"

Sàcagawea's Breadroot Binge:

The Plains tribes made wide use of the bulb of the breadroot, or "prairie apple." This bulb could be eaten raw or boiled like today's potatoes. Commonly dug from late summer until first frost, the bulbs were strung together to dry in the sun, then stored whole or pulverized into chunks of powder. After eating so little for days while she was sick, Sacagawea shocked her weakened digestive system with the feast of unripe "prairie apples."

Once I was stronger, we began the long, hard climb around the Great Thundering Falls. Where the land fell away long and flat, the men put a sail on one of the canoes. The wind blew against it so hard, the canoe raced along just as fast as if it had been on water. Sailing on dry land, they called it.

Then the storms came. They battered and bruised us. Hailstones the size of fists slammed down from the sky, knocking some senseless and tearing our clothes to rags. The sky grew black. It boiled. The wind howled like wolves.

"Run!" cried Clark. "Take shelter!" He pointed to a dry ravine. Charbonneau and I did as Clark said, thinking the overhanging rocks would keep us dry. I took the cradleboard from my back and took Pomp out. I clutched him to me, pressing my back hard against the dirt bank. Clark joined us there. But the rain came too hard and fast. Suddenly the hillsides gave way in a torrent of tumbling water, rocks, and mud.

The type of `canoe` used by the Corps of Discovery was large enough to accommodate ten adults or an abundance of cargo. It sat low in the water and could achieve respectable speeds. Off the water, however, the canoe had to be pulled by the men using wheeled frames and muscle power. At one point near the Great Falls of the Missouri, the men hoisted a sail in one of the canoes and let the wind carry it over the flat, dry land. [LIZ HAHN PHOTO.]

[ILLUSTRATION COURTESY MONTANA STATE PARKS, MISSOURI RIVER.]

Charbonneau got out first, then reached down for me. Clark was standing waist-deep in water, where no water had been before. He pushed me up to Charbonneau with Pomp in my arms, just in time. Clark barely had time to scramble up behind me before the water grew as tall as two men, then as tall as three. We lost the cradleboard, but my Pomp was safe.

The next day, we returned to see if we could find what had been lost: Clark's umbrella, Clark's compass, and the cradleboard. The compass was found in the mud, but nothing else.

Later, Clark wrote of this in his journal. He named the place "Defeated Drain," because his compass was safe. But I thought, it is we who are defeated. For in the cradleboard taken by the storm, were all of Pomp's clothes and all of my possessions.

The Corps of Discovery would have heard the deafening roar of the Great Falls of the Missouri River from many miles away, but they were completely unprepared for the sight of it days later. The long portage of canoes and supplies demanded by the Great Falls was undoubtedly one of the most physically challenging parts of the journey for the Corps.

[F. Jay Haynes photo, 1880. Courtesy of the Haynes Foundation Collection, Montana Historical Society, Helena.]

We traveled on. Slowly, I began to recognize the country. We stopped at the Three Forks where I had been taken from my people by the Minnetaree. I told the story of my capture, and Charbonneau translated my words for the white Chiefs. Then I spotted the Beaverhead Hill. I knew we were getting closer to the Agui Dika.

But many of the men were sick or injured. Lewis decided he and a few of the others would go on ahead and try to find my people. I thought surely Charbonneau and I would be allowed to go with him, since I knew the talk. These were my people. But Lewis said no; Clark and the rest of us would stay here until all could follow.

First, though, Lewis wanted to know what was the word for "white man" in Shoshoni. There wasn't one. But to say nothing would have been disrespectful.

"Tell him ta-vai-bon-e," which meant the same as "stranger." It was as close as I could think of.

The Obsidian-bladed knife (reproduction pictured) has an elk antler handle. Projectile and blade points were often hand-formed from chert, flint, or agate.
[Terry McGrew photo. McGrew Photography. © Joyce Badgley Hunsaker and Towanda, Inc.]

Instead I told Charbonneau, "Tell him ta-vai-bon-e," which meant the same as "stranger." It was as close as I could think of. And surely these men with their faces the color of ash would be considered strangers by my people.

One of the men going with Lewis knew the sign talk, so he could make himself understood. Lewis himself knew to make welcome signals with his blanket, waving it in the air, then spreading it on the ground as if for trade or council. I told Charbonneau, "Tell him to paint the cheeks of the women red, as a sign of peace." Then they were gone.

Short black lines on the wool **Hudson Bay Company blanket** were referred to as "points," indicating the blanket's value. In his journals, Lewis refers to "capotes"—long, hooded coats made from these Hudson's Bay blankets—that kept his men as warm and comfortable as was possible during the wet Fort Clatsop winter.

[TERRY MCGREW PHOTO, MCGREW PHOTOGRAPHY. © JOYCE BADGLEY HUNSAKER AND TOWANDA, INC.]

It was seven sleeps before we caught up to them. I will never forget entering into the camp of the Agui Dika. First, I smelled the smoke of the tanning fires. Then, I heard the familiar sounds of dogs barking and children laughing. I danced with excitement and sucked my fingers to tell Clark these were, indeed, the people of my childhood.

The dogs ran out to meet us first, snarling and yelping and sniffing at our ankles. Then came the proud, young men, every inch warriors. Finally came the women with their children. Lewis and the head men of the camp strode forward. Lewis's face was covered with red paint. He had shells tied in his hair, a mark of honor. The men embraced Clark so many times, soon all were smeared with grease and paint. "The national hug," Lewis called it.

Each tribe had its own moccasin style. The pair shown here is of typical Shoshoni construction and design, circa 1900.
[TERRY McGREW PHOTO, McGREW PHOTOGRAPHY. © JOYCE BADGLEY HUNSAKER AND TOWANDA, INC.]

The women closed around me. They began to dance. They began to sing.

"Sai! Sai!" they sang. "Ah-hi-e! It is good."

I held my son out to them.

"Behold the faces of your grandmothers," I told Pomp. "Numa. These are The People."

My eyes went from one face to another. Then I saw her. No, it could not be! But then she smiled. There could be no mistake. Naya Nuki! My friend! She was alive! She had found our people after all! We clung to one another's necks and cried and cried and cried. We both had thought the other dead, walking with spirits. Yet we had both survived!

The men went off together. We women did the same, talking all at once and touching one another. It had been so long since I had heard this much Shoshoni spoken at one time, I do not remember now all that was said.

The women closed around me. They began to dance. They began to sing. "Sai! Sai! Ah-hi-e! It is good."

Known by a variety of names by different tribes, the coyote (or prairie wolf) played a key role in storytelling and moral instruction.
[TERRY McGREW PHOTO, McGREW PHOTOGRAPHY. © JOYCE BADGLEY HUNSAKER AND TOWANDA, INC.]

All too soon, Charbonneau sent for me. It was time to talk about getting horses for crossing the Shining Mountains.

It was unusual for a woman to speak in Council, so I wrapped my blanket around me as I entered and kept my eyes down, showing respect. I took off my moccasins and tucked my legs under me, to the right, so my dress covered them. This was for modesty, in the old way.

First, Lewis spoke. The words were repeated in French; then Charbonneau said them in Hidatsa to me. I said them in Shoshoni and waited for a reply.

For a long time there was no reply. But I kept my eyes down. I waited. Finally, the one Lewis called "Chief" started to talk. I knew that voice! My head jerked up and I stared into his face. I knew I should not do this, but I could not help myself.

"Brother!"

I jumped to my feet and reached to clasp my blanket around us both, reclaiming my clan. I wept openly now.

"Brother! Brother!"

Sacagawea makes the sign of the horse. Both Sacagawea and her husband were hired by Lewis and Clark because the captains needed their skills as translators in acquiring the sturdy and sure-footed horses of the "Snake" Indians to cross the Shining Mountains. [LIZ HAHN PHOTO.]

Even in my joy, I was afraid I had shamed him—first, crying out in Council, then, showing so much feeling in front of the men. But Cameahwait's eyes showed no anger to me when I looked again, only surprise. Now, emotion flowed over me like a river too big for its banks. I could barely sit through the rest of the Council. I could barely concentrate on the words I was supposed to translate.

Emotion flowed over me like a river too big for its banks.... I could barely concentrate on the words I was supposed to translate.

Sacagawea stands wrapped in her blanket to show respect when speaking in Shoshone Council—a place where women were not normally allowed. Among most tribal peoples, the buffalo robe and the blanket had specific "languages" all their own. The manner in which each was worn signaled a precise message to those observing the wearer. [Liz Hahn photo.]

In the end, I got the horses Lewis and Clark needed for crossing the Shining Mountains. And I got my family back. So many were now dead: mother, father, sisters. But one of my sisters had left a son. I adopted him that day, as was our custom. Bazil Shoogan became my son, and I became his mother. So it would be, from that time forward.

Yet I almost got more family than I wanted. The man my father had promised me to in marriage when I was a child now came forward to claim me as his wife! He already had two wives, so when he saw I had Pomp, he decided he did not want me so badly after all. I think he did not want another small mouth to feed.

My people were starving. Game had become so scarce, they ate animals raw at the kill site, right down to the soft part of the hooves! The women dug all the roots and gathered all the berries they could find, but it was not enough. It was past time for my people to follow the buffalo. They had stayed at this camp out of respect for Lewis and Clark. Now, they could wait no longer.

And now, my path led in the other direction, across the Shining Mountains to the river the whites called "Columbia," and from there to the Big Water Where the Sun Goes Down. I left Bazil Shoogan with my brother, thinking I would reunite with him on our return trip to the Mandan Village. I could not see the future. I did not know then that my path would not cross the path of my people again on this journey. We traveled on.

Game had become so scarce, they ate animals raw at the kill site, right down to the soft part of the hooves!

Day followed day, and we began to endure what my people had endured. There was less and less game. Before, it had taken four deer every day, or an elk and a deer, or a buffalo to feed us. Now, there was next to nothing. The parched corn and "carry-soup" of Captain Lewis could not sustain us without meat. So the white men started killing the horses to eat, the same horses they had bargained so hard for with my brother. Later, they traded for dogs and ate them.

But I refused, no matter how hungry I was. Numa do not eat their dogs or their horses!

Buffalo tooth necklace (reproduction pictured). Buffalo were considered The Gift to the People, as so many parts of the animal could be used for tribal survival. Almost a supermarket, department store, and pharmacy on the hoof, the buffalo played a pivotal role in the ceremonial and everyday life of many tribal nations.

[TERRY MCGREW PHOTO, MCGREW PHOTOGRAPHY. © JOYCE BADGLEY HUNSAKER AND TOWANDA, INC.]

When we came to the Nez Perce (Nimiipu), they fed us well. It was said that at first they had decided to kill us or let us die of our own ignorance. But an old woman among them, whose name was Wetkuiis, said white traders had one time saved her life. She said now the tribe should spare ours, so the debt would be balanced. Because of her words, the Nimiipu welcomed us. They honored us. They traded many goods.

The chief, Twisted Hair, drew a map on white elk skin of the rivers flowing west. It was decided to leave our horses with Twisted Hair's band until we came back from the Big Water. Lewis told his men to start building canoes.

Word traveled fast of our coming once we were back on the rivers. Drumming and singing followed us down to the Columbia, then toward the Big Water. Sometimes the man Cruzatte played his fiddle in return, though it sounded more like a wounded animal than music.

+—＝◆＝—+

Brain-tanned deer hide was widely used to make carry-all bags for both sexes. This loop-strapped buckskin bag was designed to be hung from a belt, so it was probably intended for a woman.

[TERRY MCGREW PHOTO, MCGREW PHOTOGRAPHY. © JOYCE BADGLEY HUNSAKER AND TOWANDA, INC.]

The captains continued to buy dogs to eat, for the tribes on the Columbia did not want to sell us their good salmon, and the old salmon made us sick. Lewis's big black dog was still with us. Its hair was matted, and it was covered with fleas. It stank. I wondered why the captains did not eat this dog. It was so big, it would have fed many. But that never happened.

Then came the day we could hear the Big Water booming . . . booming . . . booming.

Trade beads and sash (reproduction pictured). Glass beads and brightly colored woven textiles were favored trade items among tribal people long before Lewis and Clark. Some of the first documents written about European contact with what was then called "The New World" note the trading of glass beads and red cloth to the "Indians." As trading routes pushed into our country's interior, so did the demand for trade goods such as these.
[TERRY MCGREW PHOTO, MCGREW PHOTOGRAPHY. © JOYCE BADGLEY HUNSAKER AND TOWANDA, INC.]

"Pacific!" cried Lewis.

Here we found many tribes already wearing white men's clothes and speaking white men's words. There was even, among them, a tribesman who had hair of a darker red than Clark's and marks upon his face that the captains called freckles. These tribes made hard bargains for the goods we needed. They were better Yankee traders than the Yankee traders, Clark said . . . just before the captains traded my belt of blue beads for a robe of sea otters Lewis wanted.

They were better Yankee traders than the Yankee traders....

The traders also brought firearms requiring powder, flint, and balls. These powder horns (reproductions pictured) are made from animal horn and carved wood.

[TERRY MCGREW PHOTO, MCGREW PHOTOGRAPHY. © JOYCE BADGLEY HUNSAKER AND TOWANDA, INC.]

By now, winter was closing in. The rains grew stronger. We had to build a fort in which to live until spring. But where? A vote was taken. Every man had his say, even Charbonneau. Even York, the slave man. Even me. I said we should build wherever there would be enough roots to dig. But the others decided on another place.

No Salmon for Sale: The time of year the Expedition traveled down the Columbia River is important in realizing why the tribes did not want to sell their "good" salmon. Winter was coming. This was the time of preparing and laying by of foods that would ensure the tribes' survival until the return of the salmon the next spring. Salmon swim upriver only seasonally and are not the limitless source of food the captains may have assumed they were. The journals comment on the overwhelming stench of the fish being prepared for winter. There was smoked fish, dried fish, boiled fish, and pounded fish. The tribes cannot be faulted for their survival instinct; they knew what a long Pacific Northwest winter was like. The captains did not.

Asked to vote on where to position a winter fort (which would later become known as Fort Clatsop), Sacagawea opted for a spot where *potas* were plentiful. Scholars today believe she was referring to wappato roots (shown here in a bark basket), commonly dug and processed in marshy areas throughout the Pacific Northwest. Wappato grows in the mud of shallow water and is harvested with the toes. Once dislodged, the egg-sized tubers float to the top of the water, are gathered by hand, then roasted, boiled, or dried. They were, and continue to be, used very much like potatoes. Also called arrowhead and tule potato, this bland but nutritious root was a staple of the coastal peoples' diets. The word "wappato" comes from Chinook jargon.

[COURTESY OF USDA FOREST SERVICE, LEWIS AND CLARK NATIONAL HISTORIC TRAIL INTERPRETIVE CENTER, GREAT FALLS, MONTANA.]

Fort Clatsop, they called it when it was built. It was dark. It was cold. It was always wet. We were covered with fleas. It was hardship upon hardship and want upon want. Charbonneau, Pomp, and I finally had our own sleeping place away from the others, but we suffered the same lack as everyone else. Even though many tribes visited us at the fort, we were not happy. We had very little left to trade for what we needed, and men were growing sick on the lean elk we ate every day.

Smaller than Fort Mandan, Fort Clatsop (re-creation pictured) nonetheless provided some relief from the astonishingly wet winter of 1805–1806. The journals note that during the entire four and a half months spent at Fort Clatsop, only twelve days were without rain; the sun appeared on a mere six of those twelve. This full-sized replica of Fort Clatsop was built in the 1950s using Clark's plan.

Even on the day of Christmas, which Charbonneau said was a white man's feast day, we had only spoiled elk, spoiled fish, and a few roots to eat. Gifts of tobacco and handkerchiefs were given among the men. I gave to Clark the tails of twenty-four white weasels to ornament his clothing, as befitted a leader. But it was hard to stay happy as our stomachs rumbled.

Today called ermine, white weasels were valued for their dramatic coloring during Sacagawea's time. All-white animals were rare (even those with black tips). Tribal leaders and men of high standing often wore white weasels as ornamentation on their clothing or in their hair. When Sacagawea gave a Christmas gift of twenty-four weasel tails to Clark, she may well have been showing her high regard for him as a leader. [LIZ HAHN PHOTO.]

Not long after, word came that a Great Fish had washed up on the shore of the Big Water. They said this Great Fish was as big as a river, as big as a mountain! Clark and twelve of the men were going to find it, to bring back some whale meat and oil. Charbonneau told me we were to stay behind at the fort.

I thought this very hard. Hadn't I come all this way to see the Big Water? Hadn't I endured everything the others had endured, just the same? And now there was this Monstrous Fish to be seen—and still, I would not be allowed to go?

I spoke of this to my husband in such a way and to such an extent that he could no longer pretend to be deaf. So he spoke to the captains, and finally—yes—the captains reconsidered. I would be allowed to go.

How can I tell you of this thing? Have you ever seen the Big Water? The sky comes down, as far as the eye can see, to float upon the face of the Lake with No Ending. The sky and the water almost become one—far, far away.

[ORIGINAL ART BY ERICA THURSTON.]

Then I saw the bones of the Great Fish, anchored by the sand. Waves slapped, slapped, slapped up all around them, making foam that broke into little bundles and piled up on the shore. All was so big and vast, I knew if I told my people what I had seen that day, they would say it could not be so. They would say it must be a Vision. Or they would say it must be a lie. So I put the memory into my heart, for reminding Pomp later of what he, too, had seen that day.

Too soon, it was time to return to the fort. One day was the same as the next: making salt, sewing hides, making moccasins—over three hundred pair—and trying to dry out all that was dripping. Every day it rained . . . hailed . . . thundered . . . or stormed. Tempers grew short. We were all anxious for spring to come so we could begin our journey home.

Shortly after Christmas 1805, the members of the Expedition established a salt works on the Pacific Coast (re-enactment pictured). They built a salt cairn about fifteen miles from Fort Clatsop, near present-day Seaside, Oregon. Here they boiled ocean water, accumulating roughly twenty gallons of salt by the end of February. Some of this salt was consumed, some was used to preserve deer and elk meat, and twelve gallons were packed into ironbound kegs for use on the return journey.

[Courtesy of Fort Clatsop National Memorial-National Park Service.]

Finally, it was time. Pomp was just over one year old. We left Fort Clatsop and traveled back the way we had come. Sometimes we rode in the canoes; sometimes we walked. We stopped at the camps of many tribes who remembered us.

Chief Lewis's big black dog was captured from our camp one night and taken toward a nearby village. Lewis was very angry and sent some of the men to rescue it. The dog was returned, but after that, extra guards were always posted.

At the camp of Chief Twisted Hair, we reclaimed the horses we had left with him. We dug up the caches of supplies we had buried along the way. Lewis and Clark made more speeches. Dances were held in our honor. One night, young men from the tribes even set fire to the trees to melt the snow and bring us good weather for traveling. Like fireworks on Independence Day back in the United States, Clark told us.

The brass fire starter contained flint and steel; struck one against the other, they created a spark. To encourage the spark to flame, pre-charred fabric was carried in the fire starter. If all else failed, the magnifying glass in the fire starter's lid was used to focus the sun's rays onto tinder.

[TERRY McGREW PHOTO, McGREW PHOTOGRAPHY. © JOYCE BADGLEY HUNSAKER AND TOWANDA, INC.]

Then at The Time of the Long Grass, we broke apart. Lewis took some of the men and went north along the river he named Marias. Clark and the others took fifty horses and went a different way, toward the Three Forks and the river called Yellowstone. Charbonneau, Pomp, and I went with Clark. We would meet again with Lewis in the Berry Moon on the Big River Missouri.

But ours was not an easy way. The horses' feet were so sore we had to put moccasins made of raw buffalo hide over their hooves. Wolves stole our drying meat from the scaffolds. We were chased by bears. Beaver slapped their tails all night against the water; it was impossible to sleep. And mosquitoes were so thick the men could not even see the muzzles of their guns to shoot! Pomp's face swelled to twice its size with mosquito bites, and he became very sick from their poison. We were all miserable.

Early Self-Storage: Caches are deep storage pits dug into hillsides or other protected areas where chances of remaining undisturbed were greatest. Typically, they were lined with rocks, branches, and other leafy organics. Once filled with the goods being cached, the original soil from the hole was shoveled on top to seal it. The ground surface was then restored as much as possible, in hopes no one would detect the disturbance. Everything—from foodstuffs to tobacco, pelts to muskets, and clothing to scientific specimens—was hidden in this way, with the intent that the Corps would retrieve them on the return trip. The cache storage method was unreliable, however, and the Corps lost many items when some of their caches seeped or flooded.

The fish weir, or trap, was constructed from thin willow branches that were secured by twining around the "hoops" and nose. The weir was generally placed in the water with the open end against the current. The weir's operating principle relied on the fish swimming into the opening to be trapped by the current against the weir's nose. The weir was then scooped out of the water.

[COURTESY USDA FOREST SERVICE, LEWIS AND CLARK NATIONAL HISTORIC TRAIL INTERPRETIVE CENTER, GREAT FALLS.]

At last we came to a tall rock towering above the river. We knew it must have been a sacred place, for it was covered with markings and piles of stones. Clark climbed on top. He shouted down that behind us he could see the Shining Mountains; in front of us, a prairie filled with buffalo, elk, and grass.

When he climbed down, he cut his name into the rock. Under that, he carved the day: July 25, 1806. Then he named the place Pompey's Tower, after my Pomp.

Named "Pompey's Tower" in 1806 in honor of Sacagawea's toddler, this sandstone monolith is now known as Pompey's Pillar. Its shape and impact remained essentially unchanged during the hundred years between Clark's naming of it and the photographer's recording of its image here.

[L.A. Huffman photo, 1902. Courtesy of the Montana Historical Society, Helena.]

By the Berry Moon, we met again with Lewis and the others at the Big River. We saw the others in the boats, but where was Lewis? He was nowhere to be seen. Had something happened to the Great Chief? He was finally found lying on his stomach in one of the boats. He had been shot in his sitter by the fiddleman, Cruzatte.

"We were hunting! I thought you were an elk!" Cruzatte told Lewis. "I only have one good eye!" But some of the men wondered if it had been an accident after all.

Lewis said his wounds would be better before the next moon. He wanted Clark to help him sit upright in the boat for entering the great Mandan villages. This was done.

We entered together into the place which had been our beginning. Charbonneau was paid five hundred dollars for his part in the Journey of Discovery, as had been agreed. He got not one penny extra for me. Then it was time for the captains to go. They must continue downriver until they reached the Great Father.

The abalone shell used to make these hair ornaments was highly prized by inland tribes for personal decoration and ceremonial use. Commonly traded by coastal tribes, the shell became more valuable each time it changed hands toward the Rocky (Shining) Mountains and the plains.

[TERRY MCGREW PHOTO, MCGREW PHOTOGRAPHY. © JOYCE BADGLEY HUNSAKER AND TOWANDA, INC.]

43

Clark came to us as we watched the canoes being readied. He made my husband what he thought was a generous offer. "Give Pomp to me," said Clark. "He will live in my house in the United States. I will send him to school. He will learn white men's ways. He will be my son." I knew Clark felt affection for Pomp. But how could I let him go? My dancing boy had barely found his legs. He was not even weaned. No! Pomp was my son! He would stay with me! I told my husband, "You tell Clark no!"

Charbonneau turned to Clark and said, "Yes. When the boy is older we will send him to you. He will be your son." The two men clasped their hands in agreement.

I stood on the bank of the river, holding onto Pomp. Lewis and Clark's canoes were going one way—white trappers' and traders' canoes were going the other. Yet I knew they were all going to the same place: to the Land of Tomorrow.

This was the end of my journey; this was the beginning of a Great Change.

Statue of
Sacagawea
and Pomp.

[STATE HISTORICAL
SOCIETY OF NORTH
DAKOTA; R. REID
PHOTO.]

This was the end of my journey; this was the beginning of a Great Change. I understood that what I had seen—the lands I had passed through, the lands of my people and others like them—would never again be the same.

I tell you these things that they may be remembered with truth and respect.

Ah-hi-e! It is good that you remember.

Sacagawea motions the two directions the white men were traveling—Lewis and Clark were headed home, but more white trappers and traders were headed into the western frontier from which Sacagawea had just returned. The "Great Change" had begun.
[Liz Hahn photo.]

Summary

Sacagawea's journey with the Corps of Discovery lasted only sixteen months. Yet we consider her epic as among the most heroic of our American historical tales. What happened after she returned to the Mandan and Hidatsa villages? Did she have to send Pomp to William Clark, as her husband promised? Did she have other children? When did she die, and where?

Yes, Sacagawea sent Pomp to Clark when Pomp was older. Charbonneau had given his word; it was Sacagawea's duty to abide by the agreement. She also sent a young daughter, Lizette (who was born a few years after the expedition), along with Otter Woman's son, Toussaint. Of the three children, only Pomp was formally adopted by Clark. The other two children fade from historical record after that.

Most non-tribal historians today agree that Sacagawea herself died only six years after the expedition from "putrid fever" at Fort Manuel Lisa, a fur-trading post where Charbonneau was staying at the time. William Clark—who was then Director of Indian Affairs—believed this when it was reported to him, and he recorded in his journal "Sacagawea, dead."

Many tribal historians, however, disagree. They say there is much oral history that says Sacagawea lived a very long time. They say that she finally left Charbonneau and lived among her tribal relatives until reunited with her adopted son, Bazil Shoogan, on the Wind River Reservation in present-day Wyoming. There is a gravestone on the reservation today that says Sacagawea is buried there.

Ultimately, it is a mystery. Until DNA technology can catch up to our curiosity about this extraordinary woman, we will never know for sure.

About the Author

Joyce Badgley Hunsaker is an award-winning historical interpreter and storyteller. Her thoughtful and carefully researched programs have won her national acclaim as both actress and historian. For more than twenty years, she has presented her living histories from around wilderness campfires to the halls of the U.S. Congress. She has performed across the country with symphonies, in schools, universities, museums, on national television and radio, and with the NBA Portland Trailblazers. Her program about Sacagawea was performed by invitation at the 2002 Winter Olympics.

Other "command performances" have included such distinguished audiences as the Smithsonian Institution, Disney, the National Geographic Society, the Nature Conservancy, The Public Lands Foundation, and Russian Educational Television. Ms. Hunsaker's living history dramas and books are currently being used in Russia to teach American history and English.

Joyce Badgley Hunsaker's family bloodlines include Cherokee and Sioux, English, French, and Scots-Irish. Several tribes have honored her with ceremonial names. She was born at the base of the Elkhorn Mountains in remote northeastern Oregon and for forty years lived within sight of Sacajawea Peak in Chief Joseph's "Land of the Winding Waters." Now, she and her husband, David, reside in the red rock country of southern Utah.

Photography of "Sacagawea" Disclaimer

Photography had not been invented by 1805–1806, so no photographs exist showing what Sacagawea really looked like when she was on her epic adventure. All photographs in this book of a real woman dressed in tribal regalia are of the author portraying Sacagawea in the living history presentation called "Sacagawea Speaks."

Also Available:

Sacagawea Speaks: Beyond the Shining Mountains with Lewis & Clark

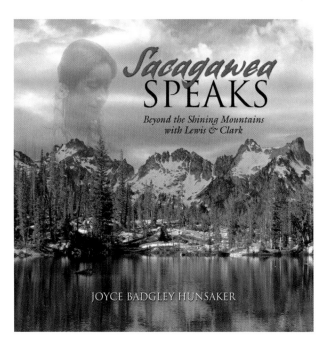

For more detailed information about Sacagawea and the Corps of Discovery, see our parent book, *Sacagawea Speaks: Beyond the Shining Mountains with Lewis & Clark* (The Globe Pequot Press, $27.50 cloth, ISBN 1-58592-079-7). Available in *Sacagawea Speaks* are timelines, biographical sketches of expedition members, Shoshoni vocabulary, era weaponry guides, expedition supply lists, and a full complement of endnotes. Perfect for teachers, researchers, or libraries. To order, call (800) 243–0495.

Sacagawea Speaks was honored as 2001 History Book of the Year by *ForeWord* magazine.

They Call Me Sacagawea
Copyright © 2003 by Joyce Badgley Hunsaker

Cover image of Sacagawea (Joyce Badgley Hunsaker portraying Sacagawea) by Liz Hahn. Cover artifact images are found with complete captions within the book, all photos by Terry McGrew, McGrew Photography.
Cover and text design by Ginger Knaff, GingerBee Creative

Library of Congress Cataloging-in-Publication Data is available.

ISBN 0-7627-2580-X

Printed in Canada
First Edition/First Printing